Nonprofit Quick Guide™

How to Run an Annual Business Appeal

Linda Lysakowski, ACFRE
Joanne Oppelt, MHA

Nonprofit Quick Guide: How to Run an Annual Business Appeal

One of the **Nonprofit Quick Guide**™ series

Published by Joanne Oppelt Consulting, LLC

Copyright © 2021 by Joanne Oppelt and Linda Lysakowski

ISBN Print Book: 978-1-951978-15-0

13 12 11 10 9 8 7 6 5 4 3 2 1

Printed in the United States of America

About the Authors

LINDA LYSAKOWSKI, ACFRE

Linda is one of approximately one hundred professionals worldwide to hold the Advanced Certified Fundraising Executive designation. Linda is the author of ten nonfiction books, a contributing author, co-editor, or co-author of twenty others. She has also written six books unrelated to the nonprofit world.

Linda has more than thirty years in the development field. She worked for a university and a museum before starting her own consulting firm. In her twenty-five years as a philanthropic consultant, Linda has managed capital campaigns that have raised more than $50 million, helped hundreds of nonprofit organizations achieve their development goals, and trained more than forty thousand development professionals in most of the fifty states of the United States, Canada, Mexico, Egypt, and Bermuda.

She served on the Association of Fundraising Philanthropy (AFP) Foundation for Philanthropy Board and on the Professional Advancement Division for AFP. She is a past president of the Eastern Pennsylvania and Sierra (Nevada) AFP chapters. She received the Outstanding Fundraiser of the Year award from the Eastern Pennsylvania, Las Vegas, and Sierra (Nevada) chapters of AFP, was honored with the Barbara Marion Award for Outstanding Service to AFP and received the Lifetime Achievement Award from the Las Vegas AFP chapter.

Linda is a graduate of Alvernia University with majors in banking and finance as well as theology/philosophy, and a minor in communications. As a graduate of AFP's Faculty Training Academy, she is a Master Teacher.

Joanne Oppelt, mha

Joanne, principal of Joanne Oppelt Consulting, LLC, is a seasoned rainmaker with a distinguished track record of success. During her twenty-five-plus years working in the nonprofit arena, she built or rebuilt successful fundraising departments at every stop, helping her organizations grow capacity and more effectively fulfill their missions.

She has held positions from grantwriter to executive director at the nonprofits Community Access Unlimited, Caring Contact: A Listening Community, Family to Family Network of New Jersey, Christian Healthcare Center, March of Dimes Central New Jersey, Prevent Child Abuse New Jersey, and Maternal and Family Health Services. Her extensive background in a variety of work roles and organizations enables her to understand the realities and challenges nonprofit practitioners face–both internally and externally. Her success at every stop positions her to help any nonprofit, whether through her books or consulting practice, turn around its struggling fundraising operations.

Joanne is the author of four books and co-author of eight. She has taught at Kean University as an Adjunct Professor in its graduate program. She is also a highly sought-after speaker and presenter.

Joanne holds a master's degree in health administration from Wilkes University, where she graduated with distinction. Her bachelor's degree is in education, with a minor in psychology.

Dedication

To all the businesses who build stronger communities through their contributions of money, products or services. and employee volunteers to the nonprofits in their communities.

Contents

Chapter One

What Is the Best Way to Approach Businesses?

How do you approach your business community?

For many organizations, the answer is, "We don't!" For others, it is seeking sponsorship of their events. Some apply for corporate foundation grants. Or perhaps they call their local businesses when they need gifts in kind or maybe for a gift certificate for their silent auction. Some have even joined their local chamber of commerce, gotten the mailing list, and sent a letter to member businesses (horrors!).

What's wrong with all these methods?

First, let's talk about corporate sponsorship. So many businesses are tired of sponsoring events. They get a table at your gala and then have to fill that table, deciding who from their business should attend. And don't forget every nonprofit in your community is probably holding a gala. Or, you ask them to sponsor a hole at your golf tournament. "Big deal," they think, "we can get exposure to the seventy-two people who will be playing golf that day." Or they sponsor a run, walk, bowling day, or the like. Again, not a great bargain for companies. People are there to run, walk, bowl, play tennis, whatever the activity, not because they care about your mission, and certainly not to see which companies are involved. Many businesses have changed their sponsorship activities to discourage all the events. Special events cause donor and sponsor fatigue and are not the best return on investment (ROI) for either the nonprofit or the company. There are other less costly, more beneficial ways to achieve both your goals. And businesses know all about ROI. That's how they make their money. They want to partner with nonprofits that are aware of ROI. They want the most bang for their buck and gravitate to nonprofits who have thought about the best way to give it to them.

Corporate foundation grants can be very good for a nonprofit, but remember that only 5 percent of businesses in the United States are corporations, and not all of them have foundations. So, yes, seek those grants when they are available, but don't let your approach to businesses end there. Remember, the other 95 percent of businesses are LLCs, partnerships, sole proprietors, or Subchapter S corporations.

Gifts in kind can also be useful but do the businesses offer what you need? Do the gifts in kind offset your budget? If not, they can become a nightmare when you try to unload a thousand pairs of purple pantyhose (yes, that was really offered to a charity—and accepted by them, for some strange reason), or a gift of a warehouse full of lead-based paint. Be very careful; you really do need to look a gift horse in the mouth.

Another risk you run—and we've seen this happen—is that someone from your organization solicits a local business for a gift certificate for a $50 dinner, for example, and maybe you were planning to approach that restaurant chain for a $1,000 donation. You must coordinate all of your agency efforts when it comes to fundraising.

Then there is the fatal mistake of trying to do a direct mail campaign to businesses. How many times do you think that letter actually reaches the company's decision-maker(s)? Pretty slim chance of that happening unless it is a sole proprietor! Even trying to get the decision-maker made by phone or email is hard because of the gatekeepers involved.

So, what's left?

Personal solicitation. But, how do you get in the door to see the right people? Well, first, you have to determine who are the right businesses to approach. We'll talk about identifying business donors in **Chapter Two**.

Planning an Annual Appeal with Volunteer Business Leaders

You will be amazed at how many more businesses you can visit working with volunteers who are part of the community you want to solicit the business community. They will be able to open doors to corporate leaders you might not have access to on your own. Of course, they also provide many sets of extra hands and feet, ears to listen, and mouths to ask. And they will be able to access gifts from their own companies. You can even get gifts from them as volunteers. Think of all the money you can raise then!

Obviously, there is a lot to consider in asking for contributions from the business community. So, let's look at how you can successfully pull this off *this year*.

Wrapping It Up

◆ Many businesses do not want to sponsor special events because they know that does not show the most ROI for either them or the nonprofits they want to help.

◆ Gifts in kind can be great, but do they really offset your budget? And are they items you can really use?

◆ Most people who attend runs, walks, golf tournaments, and the like are there because they enjoy the activity, not to look at who the event sponsors are. Plus, these types of events give limited exposure to businesses.

◆ Direct mail is not the best way to solicit the business community.

Chapter Two

Finding Prospective Business Donors

For most people, getting in the door is often the most challenging part of making an ask. And it is really intimidating for those who have not worked in the corporate world. Making cold calls is usually not very productive, so the first step is to find businesses and business leaders who have a connection to your organization or are likely to be interested in what your organization does for the community.

You might want to begin with vendors, companies your board or staff members are connected to, businesses in your neighborhood, or companies or leaders who have a natural affiliation with your mission—for example, a toy manufacturer or distributor if your organization serves children. Do some brainstorming at staff, board, and development committee meetings.

You can use a form like this to get the ball rolling. We suggest using it with the leaders and your colleagues on the board, your staff, and your development committee. Each of these groups has its own contacts and connections that may surprise you.

Brainstorming Form: Potential Business Donors

Your Name: _____

Category	Name & Company Name	Potential for Giving	I do Business with This Company	I am Willing to Contact this Company
My accountant				
My car dealer				

Category	Name & Company Name	Potential for Giving	I do Business with This Company	I am Willing to Contact this Company
My banker(s)				
My attorney				
Members of my profession-al association				
My insurance agent				
My doctor(s)				
My Realtor				
My dentist(s)				
Members of a service club to which I belong				
Neighbors who own busi-nesses or work for businesses				

Category	Name & Company Name	Potential for Giving	I do Business with This Company	I am Willing to Contact this Company
Relatives who own business-es or work for businesses				
Business clients/ customers of mine				

Category	Name & Company Name	Potential for Giving	I do Business with This Company	I am Willing to Contact this Company
People with whom I worship who own businesses or work for businesses				
People with whom I went to school who own businesses or work for businesses				
Parents of children with whom my children go to school who own businesses or work for businesses				

Category	Name & Company Name	Potential for Giving	I do Business with This Company	I am Willing to Contact this Company
People with whom I play sports who own business-es or work for businesses				
Businesses I know support other charities				
Other Businesses				

Once you have names, you can prioritize them. Do additional research on your top prospects. Look at the companies' websites, read their annual reports, and do web searches for press articles featuring the companies you are interested in. If you are active in a local business group or association, you can also ask for contact information.

Build a chart of possible business leaders to approach. Some of those you will likely have a connection to—perhaps their companies donated to you before, one of your board members might have a relationship with the company or the corporate leader, or maybe some of the company's employees have volunteered at your organization. But what about those you have no contact with? How do you start developing those relationships? We'll talk about that in **Chapter Three.** But for now, back to building your list. Take your previous list and look at the relationships you know about.

Company	Business Leader(s)	Any Relationship with Our Organization?	To What Groups Does This Leader Belong?	What Are This Leader's Interests?

In the "Any Relationship" column, list any possible contacts you might have, even if they are weak connections. You might be able to cultivate them into stronger ones.

To complete the "To What Groups Does This Leader Belong?" column, you might have to do some research. Attend a few meetings of your chamber of commerce and see if these leaders are in attendance—even if you do not get to meet them personally. Attend other nonprofit events and see if these leaders attend those events. Ask board members, development committee members, staff members, and other volunteers what they know about these leaders. Do they belong to Rotary or other service clubs? Do they travel a lot for business? Do they have family obligations that keep them at home most evenings? Are they involved in any civic groups? What are their interests? Do they love kids, serve as mentors, have family members with a disease your organization treats, have strong feelings about preserving the environment? Do they hunt, play golf, attend the local symphony, attend church?

Once you've developed this list, you might find stronger connections than you thought you had with some of these leaders.

Start with the contacts you have some connection to and see if you can cultivate a stronger relationship. If this leader is a Rotary member, for example, maybe you can arrange to speak to this prospect's Rotary club. If you know a leader is a regular church attender, see if anyone on your board or staff belongs to the same church. If you know the leader attends the symphony, find out which of your board members or staff might also be subscribers to the symphony.

Once you have a list of some business leaders with whom you have at least a remote connection, see if you can cultivate those relationships into something deeper—before asking their companies to support you financially.

Wrapping It Up

- First, build a list of potential businesses that might support you.
- Find out who the decision-makers/leaders of these businesses are.
- Enlist board, staff, and volunteers to help brainstorm ideas.
- Research these businesses and the leaders of the companies.

Chapter Three

How Do You Build Relationships with Business Leaders?

The first thing you need to build relationships with business leaders is to hang out where the corporate leaders hang out. You won't find them by sitting in your office. Join and get involved with groups like your local chamber of commerce.

Don't forget that many larger communities have more than one chamber.

For example, in Linda's community, there is a metro chamber, a women's chamber, an Asian-American chamber, a Latino chamber, an urban chamber, an LGBT chamber, a green chamber, and a health and fitness chamber, in addition to several suburban chambers. Find one or two that best suit your organization. You won't be able to be active in all of them! Because, to see results, you can't just join the chamber. You need to get involved, attend meetings, serve on committees, and the like if you want to meet business leaders and make an impression on them.

Once you have established initial contact, you want to learn more about the business leaders, find out about their companies, and help them learn more about your organization. Cultivation events are a great way to accomplish all three of these tasks.

A Primo Cultivation Idea

Business leaders generally will attend early-morning meetings before they go to the office. So, plan cultivation events to which they can be invited at a time convenient to them.

The first step is to identify your audience. List the business leaders you will invite to your cultivation event(s).

Business Leader	Title	Company	Address	Phone	Gatekeeper (If Available)	Email (If Available)

Now let's plan the event. If your list is long, you might want to plan several events. You will probably want to invite about twenty-five leaders to each event. You should try for a number of attendees of between ten and fifteen, but not everyone will be able to attend. Sometimes organizations organize the invitees by category—bankers and financial people, utility company leaders, high-tech company leaders, insurance company executives, and so forth.

The next step is to find a chair of the event—a business leader who will be known and respected by the list of leaders you want to invite to the event. Preferably this chair will already be familiar with and have a passion for your organization. It could be a board member, a member of your development committee, a major donor, a volunteer, or someone connected to one of your board or staff members.

Suggestions for Business Leader Breakfast Event Host

Name	Title	Business	Contact Info	Who in Our Organization Can Ask This Leader to Host the Event?

Now, prioritize the list. Who is the best person to chair the event? Second best? And so on?

Choose several dates that will work for your organization before approaching the first person on your list. When you contact this person, be sure to mention why you want them to chair the event and the event's purpose. Make it clear that you are not asking for money but for advice from those who attend this event.

Once you have a chair, let this person know you will write a letter of invitation. If the chair is willing to use company letterhead and envelopes, that will look more personal than using your organization's letterhead, and it will attract the attention of the invitees. You should accept the RSVPs at your office, though. Do not expect the chair to handle this. Share your list of invitees with the chair, and make sure everyone on the list is approved by the chair. Also, ask the chair if there are any names you should add to your list.

Plan a light meal, and keep your agenda brief. A suggested agenda would include the following:

- A brief welcome from the chair
- A brief update from your CEO explaining your programs and how you are addressing community needs
- A tour or virtual tour of your organization
- Time for questions and "advice giving"

When it comes to the open-discussion part, have some questions either written or verbally addressed to the group. Following are some examples:

- Are there community needs you think our organization should be addressing?

◆ Are there ways you think we can better market our programs to the community?

◆ Do you have an employee volunteer program? If so, would your employees be interested in volunteering in any way for us?

◆ Are there ways we might partner with your company?

Our book, ***Nonprofit Quick Guide: How to Run a Donor Cultivation Event,*** goes into more detail about planning and implementing successful cultivation events.

Once you've held your cultivation event(s), the next step is following up with attendees, particularly those who asked for more information or suggested possible partnership arrangements or employee volunteering opportunities. Do the follow-up one on one with the person who attended the event.

Track your follow-up information on a list, which will then be added to your database.

Follow-Up from Cultivation Event

Date of event: _____

Event host: _____

Attendee	Contact Info	Questions Requiring Follow-Up	Possible Volunteer Opportunity	Possible Funding Opportunity	Other

You will also want to follow up with those who did not attend the event. Make a list of those who did not attend.

Date of event: _____
Event host: _____

Invitee	Reason for Not Attending (If Known)	Invite to Future Event	Remove from List	Cultivate Individually

If many people simply did not find your first date or time convenient, you will probably want to hold a second event to accommodate them. Some of the people invited might not find any of your times convenient and might need to be contacted individually. Make a list of those you want to contact individually.

Individual Cultivation Prospects

Name	Company	Contact Information	Gatekeeper (If Known)	Person from Our Organization Who Should Schedule Appointment

When meeting with these prospects individually, schedule appointments in the prospects' offices at their convenience. Let them know you will take only thirty to forty minutes of their time. Since you can't conduct a live tour at these meetings, try to give them as much information as possible in a brief amount of time. Take some leave-behinds, like an annual report, brochure, or fact sheet. But don't expect them to read too much.

For discussion purposes, you can use the same questions used during the cultivation event. You don't want to be taking copious notes during the meeting, but as soon as you get outside the office, jot down any important notes—especially if there is any follow-up information you need to provide for each prospect. You might also invite each prospect to take an individual tour of your organization if that is appropriate.

You are now well on your way to developing a strong relationship with business leaders. You might try a few other tactics, such as asking your board members to host events in their homes if they are on friendly terms with the leaders you want to cultivate. However, many businesspeople don't like "mixing business with pleasure" and would rather keep these activities to work hours. Spouses might not be interested in hearing about something they perceive as business-related activities.

Once business leaders indicate a desire to get more involved with your organization, ask them to serve on your board's committee. Invite them to host cultivation events for their colleagues and friends. Invite them to speak on behalf of your organization or open the doors to other business leaders. You will soon find that a team of ambassadors for the business community will be willing to ask other businesses to get involved with your agency and ask for donations. These leaders might even start a "friendly competition" to see who can raise the most money!

Wrapping It Up

- Business leaders need to be cultivated and made aware of your organization before you ask them for money or to be a volunteer.
- Before knowing the prospects' interests, you can develop relationships by asking for advice rather than asking for money.
- Cultivation events or one-on-one cultivation activities can develop relationships with business leaders.

Chapter Four

Organizing Your Annual Business Appeal

So now you are ready to run an annual business appeal.

Before planning your annual business appeal, let's look at how you can successfully pull this off *this year*.

The key to success is developing a solid plan, starting with laying out your timeline.

Typical TimeLine for an Annual Corporate Appeal

Develop preliminary prospect list	Month one
Develop a case for support—annual fund	Month two
Recruit chair/vice-chair	Month three
Determine the number of teams needed—formula: five calls per worker, five team members per team	Month three
Develop campaign materials	Month three
Recruit team leaders	Month four
Prospect screening session with team leaders	Month five
Team leaders recruit teams	Month six
Calls assigned to teams	Month seven
Kickoff meeting	Month eight
First report meeting	Month eight
Second report meeting	Month nine
Clean up calls and visits	Month nine
Victory celebration	Month ten

You can optimize your chances of successful funding by coordinating your timeline with the businesses' fiscal years. The goal is to time when you will be asking for donations to be close to when companies are formulating their budgets and charitable giving allocations. Many companies operate on a calendar year, making the fall an ideal time to ask to be included in next year's budget.

Your preliminary prospect list will be refined as you recruit your volunteers. We'll talk more about the steps in recruiting volunteers in **Chapter Six.**

Case Statement

The next step is to write your case statement from the viewpoint of businesses. If you already have an organizational case for support, look at it and see if it resonates with business leaders. For example, describe your economic impact on the community, in addition to your social impact. Connect with them on their turf, where they are the most comfortable. See our book ***Nonprofit Quick Guide: Best-Kept Secrets to Engaging and Retaining Business Donors*** for more about business priorities and their performance indicators.

Your nonprofit makes more of an impact on your community than you might realize. Most nonprofits are quick to brag about the social impact they have—lives saved, people fed, children educated, diseases cured or managed, cultures shared, whatever your mission is. They often, however, fail to consider their economic impact on the community. Nonprofit leaders sometimes get caught up in the "tin-cup mentality" of fundraising and approach funders with an appeal that sounds like "poor us," "we need money; you have money; give us some," or (the worst approach) "we'll have to close our doors if we can't raise the money we need this year."

Businesses, and other donors, in fact, don't want to hear these words. They don't want whining, begging, or cajoling. They want to be part of the great work you're doing and part of solving important community issues.

Yes, you need a social impact statement that shows how you save lives, change lives, and improve your community. This social impact should be outlined in your case for support. You probably have done this through your case statement or grant proposals—or maybe both. So, we won't dwell too much on the social impact statement here.

But you also need an economic impact statement, especially for your business appeal. An economic impact statement shows the dollars your nonprofit puts back into the community, directly and indirectly.

Direct impact, for example, includes wages you pay, supplies, and equipment you buy locally, and taxes you pay. Indirect examples might include visitors drawn to your community because of the programs and services you offer and ancillary items these visitors purchase.

Direct impact items:

Let's start with the direct items since they are easier to track. You can sit down with your finance officer and go over each line item in your budget. A sample is shown below.

Item	Annual Budget for This Item
Salaries paid	
Taxes paid	
Rents paid	
Contracts with local contractor—consultant, accounting, legal, banking fees, etc.	
Equipment purchased locally—computers, medical equipment, etc.	
Supplies purchased locally—office or medical supplies, etc.	
Services purchased locally—lawn maintenance, etc.	
Other items specific to your organization:	

Indirect Impact Items

The indirect expenses might be a little harder to track, but you can always look at local government statistics. Or, if you are part of a national network of similar organizations, you might be able to get figures and statistics or even sample economic impact statements from these groups. For example, the American Alliance of Museums has samples available at aam-us.org/advocacy/resources/economic-impact statement/samples. Americans for the Arts has also done a lot of research in this area.

Some indirect impacts might include things like money you've saved taxpayers by keeping people out of jail, in school, and off the welfare rolls.

Ancillary Impact Items

Following are examples of ancillary services people might purchase.

◆ If a family attends a performance at your theater, they might also purchase the following: parking, dinner at a local restaurant before the performance, babysitting, gas for the car, a new dress, or a styling at a local salon.

◆ If you are an educational institution, the following are some things that people might purchase: books not available through your own bookstore, school supplies, and clothing.

◆ A hospital might look at the following: getting people back to work sooner through a rehabilitation program, saving employers money for unemployment claims, parking near the hospital, and hotel rooms for visiting family and friends.

◆ A human service organization might have an impact through the following: savings in the cost of incarceration for a teen rehab group, getting people off the welfare rolls by providing job training, daycare, etc., keeping the community healthy by providing free dental or medical services.

This list may include things you might not have thought about. So do some brainstorming with people directly involved with the people you serve about how your services impact people's lives, pocketbooks, and the community's pocketbook.

Calculating Community Impact

Use this form to brainstorm ideas of both social and economic impact for your nonprofit:

Program	Number of People Served in This Program	Number of Dollars Saved to Community by This Program	Number of Dollars Spent in the Community Because of This Program

Once you develop your economic impact statement, you will need to translate it into a written format. It does not have to be elaborate, but some color pie charts and photos would be a nice addition. It should be professionally designed and printed. Remember, you will be giving this to business leaders to show your organization's impact on your community's economy. You will also want to post it on your website. An excerpt from an example of an economic impact statement described in Linda's book, **Raise More Money from Your Business Community** is shown here:

More than eight hundred people have been removed from the welfare rolls as a direct result of their experience with the Mom's House program. In 1997 alone, Mom's House saved its communities over $8 million by moving people from welfare to working in a meaningful career.

This figure does not include the money put back into the economy in the form of federal, state, and local taxes paid by these new working people. Mom's House has proven over and over again that parents can choose life, that we can solve problems, and that we can do it without any financial support from government.

Wrapping It Up

◆ Show businesses both the social and economic impact your organization has on the community.

◆ Work with your staff to understand the benefits you contribute back to the community in economic terms.

◆ Measure direct, indirect, and ancillary economic benefits to the community.

Chapter Five

Organizing the Volunteer Structure

As with any volunteer efforts, you need to develop job descriptions before inviting volunteers to get involved. Following are descriptions for the chair, vice-chair, team leaders, and team members.

The chair of the campaign is critical. This person will be the "face" of the appeal, lead meetings, and inspire all the volunteers. You want to select a chair who is well known and respected by other members of the business community, who will be a good spokesperson for your organization, and who has the time and passion for your cause. The commitment of the chair will be for approximately six months.

Recall the five-to-one rule. This means that when asking volunteers to make in-person solicitation, it is important that you not ask any volunteer to make more than five in-person visits. More than five just sounds too intimidating. And remember, these are volunteers. They have jobs and lives outside your organization.

So start by figuring out how many volunteers you need, determine the number of companies you want to visit and divide by five.

The number of companies to be visited ÷ 5 = the number of volunteers needed.

How many volunteers do you need? _____

If this number is in the dozens or even the hundreds, don't run screaming just yet. You don't have to recruit all these volunteers yourself. You can work with team leaders, who will each recruit five people to serve on their team. So if you need a hundred volunteers, you only need to recruit twenty team leaders.

First, choose the right chair. You probably have someone in mind already based on the previous work you've done in this book. A board member? A development committee member? A corporate donor? Someone who has received services from your organization, such as an alumnus? Someone with whom you have a personal relationship?

Let's list some potential chairpersons:

Potential Chair	Company	Relationship with Your Organization	Person Who Should Make the Ask	Result

Now let's prioritize the list and start asking. Of course, you will have your recruitment packet in place before talking to potential chairs.

◆ Chair's job descriptions, along with job description for the other volunteers

◆ Timeline for the appeal

◆ Case for support

◆ Other supplemental materials, such as brochures about the organization

Once you have a chair recruited, you can use this same list to find a co-chair. Remember to let the co-chair know that you will expect that person to chair the appeal next year. Once you have the chair and co-chair in place, schedule a meeting with them to develop a list of potential volunteers to serve as team leaders. You can use this form for that purpose.

Potential Team Leader	Company	Relationship with Your Organization	Person Who Should Make the Ask	Result

Here are some brief descriptions of what you should expect your volunteers to do.

Annual Business Appeal Chair

The Annual Fund Business Committee raises money from local businesses and corporations to further the programs of XYZ Organization. Funds for this appeal are generally unrestricted and may include gifts in kind if they are appropriate for the organization and meet the guidelines established in the Gift Acceptance Policies of XYZ Organization. The Annual Business Appeal Committee will be involved in this fundraising effort between January and April each year. Chairpersons will be asked to serve a one-year term and have the following responsibilities:

- Identify and work closely with the vice-chair, who will assume to role of chair for the next annual business appeal, barring unforeseen circumstances
- Identify and help recruit approximately ten (the amount depends on your number of prospects) team leaders
- Assist with identification and evaluation of small- to medium-sized business prospects
- Solicit team leaders for their gifts
- Sign letters to be mailed to all prospects
- Attend and preside at kickoff meeting and report meetings
- Attend and preside at a victory celebration

You will also want to select a vice-chairperson who will work closely with the chair and move into the position of chair for the next year. Once you have the program up and running, you can find a vice-chair for the upcoming year from among the team leaders who excelled during the current year. Here is a sample job description for the vice-chair.

Annual Business Appeal Vice-Chair

The Annual Fund Business Committee raises money from local businesses and corporations to further the programs of XYZ Organization. Funds for this appeal are generally unrestricted and may include gifts in kind if they are appropriate for the organization and meet the guidelines established in the Gift Acceptance Policies of XYZ Organization. The Annual Business Appeal Committee will be involved in this fundraising effort between January and April each year. The vice-chairperson will be asked to serve a one-year term, with the understanding that they will move into the position of chair the following year and have the following responsibilities:

- ◆ Work closely with the chair, and assume their responsibilities in the absence of the chair
- ◆ Identify and help recruit approximately ten (the amount depends on your number of prospects) team leaders
- ◆ Assist with the identification and evaluation of small to medium-sized business prospects
- ◆ Assist the chair in soliciting team leaders for their gifts
- ◆ In the absence of the chair, attend and preside at kickoff meeting and report meetings
- ◆ In the absence of the chair, attend and preside at a victory celebration

Team leaders will be selected to help coordinate volunteers as your program grows. Using the five-to-one rule, the number of volunteers needed will be based on the number of prospects you have, i.e., if you have one hundred prospects, you will need twenty volunteers to call on them. Because these calls are made in person, you should not assign more than five prospects to any one volunteer. Managing twenty volunteers can be a task, so you may want to have four team leaders, each managing a team of five. Team leaders should also be known and respected in the business community and those who are able and willing to recruit a team of volunteers from their own company or other business colleagues they know. Here is a job description for team leaders.

Annual Business Appeal Team Leader

The Annual Fund Business Committee raises money from local businesses and corporations to further the programs of XYZ Organization. Funds for this appeal are generally unrestricted and may include gifts in kind if they are appropriate for the organization and meet the guidelines established in the Gift Acceptance Policies of XYZ Organization. The Annual Business Appeal Committee will be involved in this fundraising effort between January and April each year. Team Leaders will be asked to serve a one-year term and have the following responsibilities:

◆ Identify and recruit approximately five team workers
◆ Assist with identification and evaluation of business gift prospects (small-medium businesses)
◆ Solicit team members for their gifts
◆ Advise and encourage your team members
◆ Solicit approximately five businesses
◆ Attend and report at two to three report meetings

The annual business appeal is very dependent on volunteers. Peer-to-peer solicitation is the key to success. Prospects are more inclined to meet with a colleague than they are a stranger, and you don't have to waste your time trying to get past the gatekeepers. Plus, peers will know things about the prospects that you might not be aware of because they are not public knowledge. Examples include a company that has only recently become quite profitable or, conversely, that only recently sank to a tremulous financial footing. Peers will often know, too, whether the business leaders have a reason to care about your organization. And so forth.

Sometimes nonprofits worry about where they can recruit all these volunteers. We'll address that in the next chapter, but here is a job description for a volunteer team member. This is the easiest job of all because their duties and time are far more limited.

Annual Business Appeal Team Member

The Annual Fund Business Committee raises money from local businesses and corporations to further the programs of XYZ Organization. Funds for this appeal are generally unrestricted and may include gifts in kind if they are appropriate for the organization and meet the guidelines established in the Gift Acceptance Policies of XYZ Organization. The Annual Business Appeal Committee will be involved in this fundraising effort between the months of January and April each year. Team Members will be asked to serve a one-year term, may be invited to move into the position of team leaders in a future year, and have the following responsibilities:

◆ Assist with identification and evaluation of business prospects
◆ Attend kickoff meeting
◆ Make a personal or corporate gift to the appeal
◆ Solicit approximately five businesses
◆ Report results to your team leader in advance of the two report meetings

Wrapping It Up

◆ The chair of your business appeal is critical and should be a good leader, committed to your organization, and have the respect of his or her peers in the business community.

◆ The vice-chair will assume the chair's duties if and when needed and will move into the chair position the next year.

◆ Team leaders make the job of recruiting volunteers easier and will help identify prospects.

◆ Peer-to-peer solicitation is the most effective way to reach businesses, so your team members will be important.

◆ Remember the five-to-one rule. Each team member should be given no more than five prospects since they will be doing calls in person.

Chapter Six

Finding and Recruiting Volunteers

As we said earlier, your involvement with local business associations and your brainstorming and cultivation efforts will lead to the ability to recruit a top-notch chair and vice-chair who in turn will work with you to recruit some great team leaders. Remember that if you need a hundred volunteers, *you* don't have to recruit them all: that's why this structure works so well. The team leaders will recruit their own team members, so once you have the team leaders in place, you're golden!

One thing you will want to do when recruiting at each step of the way is to have a volunteer recruitment packet ready for each person you or your team leaders are approaching. Linda recalls one key community leader she went to see to ask if he would serve as a team leader. He was new in town but had been appointed the local cable company's CEO and was an up and coming community leader. Linda went to enlist him to serve as a team leader for her organization's annual business appeal. She went well armed with a notebook for him, explaining everything involved. After accepting the role of team leader, he said to Linda, "Do you know why I said yes to you and no to every other nonprofit that has approached me?" Eager to hear what her magic power was, she said, "Yes, of course." "Simple," he answered, "I've been in town all of two weeks, and at least fifteen nonprofits have knocked on my door, asking me to contribute or to serve on their board. You came with a short-term request so we can get to know each other better, and you came so well prepared, I couldn't say no." After recruiting a well-performing team and raising a significant amount of money that first year, that leader went on to chair her appeal the next year and then become a valued board member. So, what was in her magic volunteer recruitment notebook?

- The organization's case for support
- The organization's annual report

◆ The timeline for the annual business appeal
◆ A list of the board of directors
◆ A list of other business leaders who had already committed to being team leaders and the names of the chair and vice-chair
◆ A job description for the team leader role
◆ A preliminary list of business prospects

Once your team leaders have been recruited, gather them together for a meeting. Review the prospect list with them and ask if they have any suggestions for additions, deletions, and suggested ask amounts. Then, talk about recruiting their team members. If they work for a large business, they may want to develop a team of co-workers. Teams from a bank, for example, may want to start some friendly competition with other bankers. Have them share the prospect list with their team members and have each team member select the prospects with whom they have the best relationships. It is good to have each team member select more than five since there will likely be duplicates. You may have to spend some time coordinating who is the best person to call prospects that show up on multiple lists. Encourage team members to add their own prospects if they think a company is a good prospect and is not on the preliminary list. It is important to have all the prospect selection done before you hold your kickoff meetings so each team member can be given pledge cards for their prospects and be ready to make their calls immediately.

Remember, you're on a tight timeline. We suggest having the active solicitation period short—six to eight weeks at the most. It is much easier to enlist volunteers when they know the time commitment is short.

Provide each team leader with a form to return within two weeks, which gives them enough to meet with other team members and make their prospect selection.

Annual Corporate Appeal Team Selection Form

Team Leader	
Company	
Mailing Address	
Phone Number	Cell Number
Email	
Prospects Selected	

Team Member # 1 Name	
Company	
Mailing Address	
Phone number	Cell Number
Email	
Prospects Selected	
Team Member # 2 Name	
Company	
Mailing Address	
Phone Number	Cell Number
Email	
Prospects Selected	
Team Member # 3 Name	
Company	
Mailing Address	
Phone number	Cell Number
Email	
Prospects Selected	

Team Member # 4 Name	
Company	
Mailing Address	
Phone Number	Cell Number
Email	
Prospects Selected	
Team Member # 5 Name	
Company	
Mailing Address	
Phone Number	Cell Number
Email	
Prospects Selected	

As we mentioned, you will want to get these forms returned to the team leaders at least several weeks before your kickoff meeting, so you have plenty of time to cross-reference the forms. If the same names are selected by different team members, you will need to contact each of them to determine who should be assigned to each prospect. Some diplomacy will be needed to see that the prospect assignments are the "right person making the right call."

Volunteers often work best in teams, and team leaders or another team member can work with each team member to find the best ask team. Volunteers might request that someone from the organization accompany them on major asks. Yes, this will require some staff time. Still, the volunteers will do the work of making the initial contacts and scheduling the appointments so that the staff can focus its energy and time on soliciting donors who need special attention.

Who Should Make the Ask?

The right "ask team" is just as important when approaching businesses as it is when approaching major individual donors—maybe even more so. During your strategy session before the meetings, determine who should be part of the team. You may want to send two people to see a business leader. It could be two volunteers, or it could be that you might want to send the CEO of your organization or another staff person along with the volunteer who can open the door. The best rule of thumb, always: Send the person who has the best relationship with this prospective donor. Some questions to ask can help you choose your ask team.

Criteria	Examples	Names of Possible "Ask Team" Members Who Fit These Criteria
Who has a relationship with this business leader?	Business colleague, friend, relative, employee, staff member who has worked with this company, board member who plays golf with prospect	
Who does business with this company?	The CFO is the purchasing officer who has contracted with this company for janitorial services	
How much and what type of business?	Board member who has business, homeowners, and boat insurance with the protective donor insurance agency	
Who has information this prospect will likely be interested in hearing?	Physician who runs the cardiac program because we know this prospect is interested in funding our cardiac wing	
Do we have any employees of this company involved as volunteers for our organizations?	Midlevel manager from this company is on our board; the marketing department of this company sends ten employees to volunteer reading to our kids	

Wrapping It Up

◆ Team leaders should meet with their teams to review the prospect list and make corrections, additions, and deletions based on their knowledge.

◆ Give team members the opportunity to select the prospects they feel they can be successful with.

◆ It will require coordination to ensure the right team members are assigned to the prospects.

◆ A team selection is often the most successful approach.

Chapter Seven

Making the Calls

Now that you have your volunteers in place and your prospect list has been assigned, it is time to schedule the prospect visits. However, even if the team members are experienced fundraisers, you need to hold a kickoff meeting where they can receive "training." If you are not experienced at volunteer training, see if someone in your organization is, or seek a consultant who can help you.

At the kickoff meeting, you should first make sure everyone is familiar with the case for support—the mission, vision, and strategic plan of the organization, how much money are you trying to raise, what will the money be used for, and what are the ways businesses can give. If you can have a testimonial from a recipient of your services, that helps to pump up the enthusiasm for your mission and your case.

You also want to provide team members with some basics of asking for a gift. Remember the key to a successful "ask" is:

- the right person
- asking the right person
- for the right amount
- for the right project
- at the right time
- in the right way!

If you've done your homework, you have now selected the right askers for the right prospects, identified an ask amount for each prospect, and built your case to involve projects businesses would be started in supporting. The next step is determining the ask amounts.

Determining the ask amounts may be tricky the first year. But team leaders and team members can be helpful in this process for first-time givers. In the second year, it will be easier to base the ask amount on what the company gave the previous year and other research and knowledge. You may find that it is not the right time for some of your prospects, but don't let team members get discouraged. Ask them to make careful notes about what the prospect tells them, and perhaps they or a staff member can go back to this prospect later.

After team members have been doing this for a while, they will usually know when it's time to make an ask. General rules of thumb say you are ready to make an ask when the following is true:

◆ The prospect knows enough and cares enough about your cause to be motivated to give (often after attending a cultivation event).

◆ You know enough about the prospect to know how much to ask for (you've done your research).

◆ This is a good time for the prospect. (For example, if the company is ready to file bankruptcy, it is *not* a good time. If it has just declared record earnings for the quarter, it is likely a good time.)

◆ You've strategized on who should make the ask (you've held a strategy meeting with the "ask team").

◆ You have a good idea of which of your programs or projects the prospect is likely to support (more research on your part).

◆ Your ask team is comfortable making the ask (they've been trained and have rehearsed the ask).

Now, what is the right way to make the ask?

First of all, during your training, you'll want to make sure that all team members are familiar with your case for support so they can articulate your story to prospective donors. You also want to make sure that you've come up with suggested ask amounts for each prospect. This gives the team members a sense of confidence because they have a suggested amount to ask for, and with the case for support in hand, they can make a suggested project that might be of interest to the prospect.

In your team member packets, you will include a pledge card for each prospect with the name of the company filled in, which makes it easier for volunteers. Once they've asked for the gift, if it is yes, great! You've already given team members instructions on completing the pledge card, including finding out how and when the pledge will be paid.

If the answer is no, be sure to instruct your team leaders to take notes and report back to you on why the prospect cannot or will not give. Maybe the amount is not within their budget, or maybe you didn't ask for enough.

Perhaps they want a deeper involvement with your organization. Maybe the timing is bad.

By the way, a note on timing. First, check with your local United Way to see if they are doing an annual appeal to businesses so you can avoid doing yours at the same time. If you plan to do your appeal at the beginning of the year, you will get most businesses before they give out their allocated funds for the year. However, since most businesses do their budgets in the fall, you may want to send out a letter in September, reminding them that your annual appeal will be coming up in January (or whenever) so they can budget for it now.

Sometimes businesses have seasonal problems that might improve later in the year and will want a call back at a better time. Be sure the team member notes this and ask that team member if they are willing to make a call later in the year.

You can provide team members with a form like this to report back on each of their calls:

Company name: _____

Contact name:	Date of contact:
Gatekeeper name:	
Ask team:	
Type of contact: ❑ Visited in office ❑ Visited elsewhere	
Business address:	Home address:
Business email:	Home email:
Business website:	Personal website/Facebook/social media:
Business telephone: ❑ This is my preferred contact number.	Personal telephone: ❑ This is my preferred contact number.
Business cell: ❑ This is my preferred contact number.	Personal cell: ❑ This is my preferred contact number.

Contact summary: Information obtained should be as comprehensive as possible, i.e., company interest, company earnings, company plans, indications of personal interests, political or religious preference, remarks about family, hobbies, community interest, state of health, retirement plans, personality traits, degree of familiarity with the organization, attitudes, etc. (Please write clearly.)

Date of next action step:

Wrapping It Up

◆ Make sure all team members get enough training, even if they are experienced fundraisers.

◆ Give team members a packet with everything they will need— your case for support, pledge cards for each prospect, tips on making the ask, and reporting procedures.

◆ Sending a letter out in the fall, when most businesses do their budgets, will make it easier for volunteers because you've prepared the prospect.

◆ Remind team members to take valuable notes about their calls, which will help your ongoing business appeals.

Chapter Eight

Reporting

You will want to have regular report meetings for the team leaders during the duration of your appeal. Team members may attend but are not required to attend unless the team leaders cannot attend and send a team member to represent their team.

Team leaders must attend these report meetings for several reasons. First, it helps keep up morale. Getting together and sharing triumphs and challenges is always helpful. Some team leaders will have great successes to report, which encourages other team leaders. Some may have challenges, perhaps getting the appointment or getting a "no" response. Often other team leaders can share tips that have been successful for their team members.

And, of course, everyone likes to brag about their success. In fact, we like to give out incentives, perhaps to the team that brought in the first gift, the team member that got a business to increase the most over last year's amount (if you've been doing this for more than a year), maybe a team member who got a business to give for the first time. Make it fun. You don't need elaborate gifts, a coffee mug, a box of candy, etc. People just like to be singled out and have the spotlight on them for a moment.

Report meetings are also an incentive for the teams that may be a little late out of the starting gate.

What Should Your Report Meetings Look Like?

Remember, these are busy people and usually like to meet before they start their workday. We suggest perhaps a 7:30-8:30 a.m. time slot and to keep these meetings brief and upbeat. This is not the time to point out anything negative, like a team that hasn't made any calls yet. Reward the teams that do have early results. The others will get the message. And, if you have a team that is having problems, talk to these team leaders individually.

The Annual Business Appeal chair or vice-chair should welcome all the team leaders and talk enthusiastically about the progress made. The CEO of the organization should also offer encouragement and thanks for all the hard work being done and report on the fundraising news, such as grants received, other individual meals that may be going on, client success stories, etc.

Have the chair give an overall update on how much has been raised to date at each report meeting. Serve a light breakfast—bagels, fresh fruit, juice, and coffee should suffice. And, if you can get the food donated, that's a plus.

Allow each team leader to share their progress.

Make sure team leaders know they're expected to attend report meetings when they accept the job. We suggest holding meetings every other week, so if your appeal runs six weeks, you'll only need three sessions, and if your appeal runs for eight weeks, you'll need four meetings.

You may need to follow up with any team leaders who do not attend the report meeting, especially after the last one, so allow yourself time to bring in final pledge cards and report from the stragglers.

Victory Celebration

Plan a final victory celebration once you have everything tallied. This might be a luncheon or breakfast, whatever works best for your volunteers. Every team member gets invited to this celebration.

During the victory celebration, you will announce the final total and give out awards to the team leaders and team members. We suggest prizes for:

- ◆ The team that raised the most money
- ◆ The team that brought in the most pledges
- ◆ The individual team member who raised the most money
- ◆ The team that increased the most over last year (for the second and ensuing years)

For these prizes, you can have staff solicit things like gift certificates for restaurants, spas, movies, golf balls, etc. We suggest giving a token gift to every team member. One thing we've seen work is to provide each team member a coffee mug with the organization's logo filled with chocolates donated by a local candy manufacturer. We also suggest giving a special gift to the chair and vice-chair. Perhaps something personal, such as if the chair is an avid golfer, a round of golf. If they are strong supporters of the arts, concert tickets. Choose things that you know align with their interests.

Again, you want to keep this meeting positive and upbeat. Have the CEO express gratitude and update team members on how this money will help the organization. Give some concrete examples. And, if possible, have a program recipient give a testimonial of their experience with your organization's programs.

And, of course, encourage all team leaders and team members to come back next year, and invite a friend or colleague to get involved. If they have had a positive experience, they will come back year after year.

Sounds like your work is done, huh? Sorry, but it's not quite over. You will want to schedule a debriefing with the chair and vice-chair shortly after your victory celebration.

First, thank the chair and see if they will stay on in some capacity next year. (Hint: we've often seen Annual Business Appeal chairs move onto the board or a committee.) Try to keep them involved. They are perfect ambassadors. And confirm that the vice-chair is ready to step into the role of the chair next year. Review the project list and see if you need to make any adjustments—additions, deletions, corrections. Then review each team leader's performance—is there one who should be invited to co-chair next year? Are there some who should be replaced next year? Hopefully, most will be invited to return next year. Then look at individual team members, are there some who should move into team leader positions next year. And don't forget to ask the chair and vice-chair if they have any advice for the next year. Was the case strong enough? Do they have any suggestions to make the process smoother next year? What about the timing of the appeal? Do they feel they got sufficient staff support?

Wrapping It Up

- Report meetings are valuable morale builders in addition to making your job of tracking pledges and gifts easier.
- Team leaders should be made aware of the report meeting dates when they agree to serve.
- Don't forget to reward volunteers.
- Have a positive, upbeat victory celebration when the appeal is completed.

Chapter Nine

Bringing It All Together

We've talked about finding your prospects, cultivating them, and how to structure your annual business appeal. We've also covered the importance of recruiting, training, and maintaining your business appeal volunteers.

You should now be well on your way to a powerful business annual appeal this year. As a final note, let's set a goal.

Amount raised last fiscal year from businesses: $_____

Goal for next fiscal year from businesses: $_____

New business to approach this year:

_____
_____
_____
_____
_____
_____

Current business to ask for increased gifts:

_____
_____
_____
_____

Board members who will be asked to help identify businesses and volunteers:

_____
_____
_____

Staff members who be asked to help identify businesses and volunteers:

_____

_____

_____

Number of volunteers that will be required: _____

Volunteers who will be asked to serve on the Annual Business Appeal team:

_____

_____

_____

_____

_____

Timeline:

Task	Person Responsible	Date to Be Completed
Identify prospective corporate and business donors		
Identify opportunities for businesses to support our organization		
Create an economic impact statement, cast statement, and other materials to be used in the appeal		
Develop stewardship and volunteer recognition plan, and volunteer recruitment packets		
Identify potential volunteers		
Recruit chair and vice-chair		
Recruit team leaders		
Launch annual corporate appeal—kickoff meeting		
Report meetings		
Wrap up the appeal and hold a victory celebration		

Now that you've outlined it, it seems pretty simple, doesn't it? Guess what? It really is! Yes, it takes time! Yes, it takes good organizational planning! Yes, it takes support from your board and staff! But, once you have all this, you can do it!

Yes, you'll have to devote some time to this. Yes, some volunteers will disappoint you. Yes, some businesses will not give. Yes, you will learn by trial and error. But if you start today, you can run a successful annual business appeal and raise more money from your business community this year. And guess what? It gets better each year.

www.ingramcontent.com/pod-product-compliance
Lightning Source LLC
Chambersburg PA
CBHW071520210326

41597CB00018B/2822